About

We were on a family trip, when one morning, my nieces and nephews began asking for special pancakes. So, I jotted down their ideas and started to wonder how to bring their treats to life. A couple of quick sketches later and some tests on the hot griddle... BAM. I was ready!

While the other parents were asleep and the kids were playing, I drew a few different shapes onto the griddle. A dinosaur for the nephew, a smiling face for the neice, and a heart for my daughter. I called them all to the breakfast table and presented them with their personal creations. Instantly, smiles overtook their faces while their plates became busy with forks of hunger. Although I thought it would satisfy them for a while, I was quickly given many new requests. For the rest of the trip, I stayed busy creating more smiles with every new pancakes creation.

Hi, I'm Big Daddy, a single father who enjoys making creative and healthy meals for my family. There is nothing better than being able to put a smile on my kid's face. Isn't that what life is all about? So, I decided to create a cookbook to help anyone become a kitchen hero. I worked on many techniques and tried a few different batters – the best results are in this book to hopefully help and guide you every step of the way. Your technique and style will only improve with practice, so always keep trying and don't give up. Also, don't be afraid to mess up – you can always eat your mistakes. :) Most importantly, this is a great chance for you to capture lasting memories with your child. Trust me, they will never forget.

Make someone special smile, everyday.

How to Create Pancake Shapes

Dinos, Sports & Emojis Edition

Volume 2

Written & Illustrated
by Paul Kaiser

Equipment

6

Pantry

7

Recipe

9

Technique

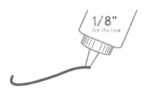

10, 11

Rex

15

Tri

16

Steggs

17

Bronto

18

Ptera

19

Bones

20

Cracked

21

Football

22

Hockey

24

Bowling

25

Basketball

26

Tennis

27

Trophy

28

More Sports

29

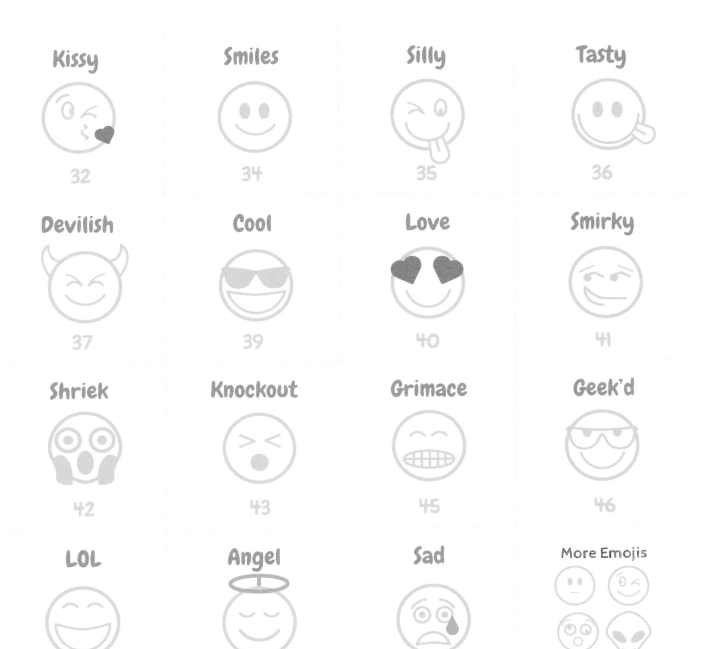

Kissy

32

Smiles

34

Silly

35

Tasty

36

Devilish

37

Cool

39

Love

40

Smirky

41

Shriek

42

Knockout

43

Grimace

45

Geek'd

46

LOL

46

Angel

46

Sad

46

More Emojis

47

Tips & Tricks

48

Notes

50

For more techniques and videos,
check often below at:

www.bigdaddypancakes.com

Equipment

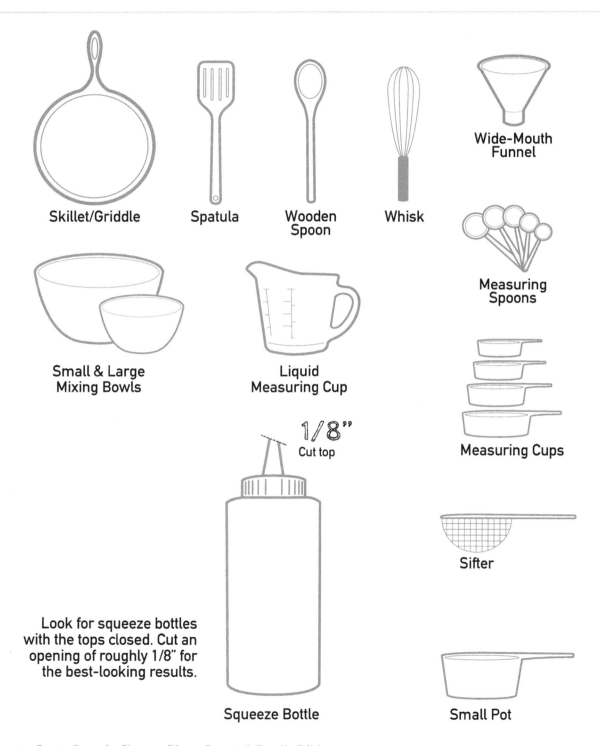

Skillet/Griddle

Spatula

Wooden Spoon

Whisk

Wide-Mouth Funnel

Measuring Spoons

Small & Large Mixing Bowls

Liquid Measuring Cup

Measuring Cups

1/8"
Cut top

Sifter

Look for squeeze bottles with the tops closed. Cut an opening of roughly 1/8" for the best-looking results.

Squeeze Bottle

Small Pot

Pantry

The DRY Ingredients

All-Purpose Flour

Baking Soda

Baking Powder

Sugar

Salt

extra flavor

Nutmeg

Cinnamon

Pumpkin Spice

The WET Ingredients

Unsalted Butter

Buttermilk

Vanilla Extract

Large Eggs

Basic
Recipe

Creates roughly
8 characters

Step ONE - DRY Ingredients

Sift the following ingredients through a sifter, into a large bowl.

- O 2 cup   All-Purpose Flour
- O 2 TB   Baking Soda
- O 2 TB   Baking Powder
- O 2 TB   Sugar
- O Pinch   Salt

Add a little spice in your mix, try one, (or all) of these.
Sometimes adding a little extra flavor can add to the season.

- O 1/4 tsp Nutmeg
- O 1/4 tsp Cinnamon
- O 1/4 tsp Pumpkin Spice

Step TWO - WET Ingredients

Melt the butter in a small pot. Allow it to cool a few minutes,
then combine in a bowl with buttermilk and vanilla.

- O 2 TB   Unsalted Butter
- O 2+1/4 cup   Buttermilk
- O 2 TB   Vanilla Extract

Crack the eggs into the large bowl with the DRY ingredients.

- O 2 lrg   Eggs

After many recipes, we
enjoyed this basic one the most.
You can always use any batter
or box version if you choose.

It's time to get creative
and have fun!

Step THREE

Pour the WET ingredients into the large mixing bowl of DRY
ingredients. Fold the mixture together with a wisk or wooden
spoon and remove the lumps. If the batter is too thick, add
1 TB Milk until the consistency is just right and smooth.
Then, pour the batter into the squeeze bottles. This can be
done carefully without a funnel, but using one may help.

- O Fold, Stir & Create

Griddle Techniques

The Line Squeeze

To make precise lines consistently, use a bottle with a small 1/8" opening. This size helps to define the shape as the heat cooks the batter. You don't need to go fast with your lines – nice steady, slow, clean lines do the job.

1/8"
For the LINES

Too Thin

Perfect

Too Thick

Remember, the batter will expand as it cooks.

Follow The Lines

The dotted lines show what to do during each step along the way.

The Process

Pour the batter to fill the large areas. To add a unique touch to your masterpiece, leave some of the areas like the eyes, nose and mouth open.

Draw

Cover

Flip

In order for your design to hold its shape and look nice, you must give the batter time to cook and set to a deeper color. We found 30 seconds to be a good rule. You can adjust timing based on the temperature of your griddle.

The Size

The average pancake is about 7" in diameter. So think about the size of your space ahead of time and realize how big you want to make your character. It will take a few tries to get used to how far apart to keep the features. Once you master the distance, it will be more simple and fun than a plain circle pancake!

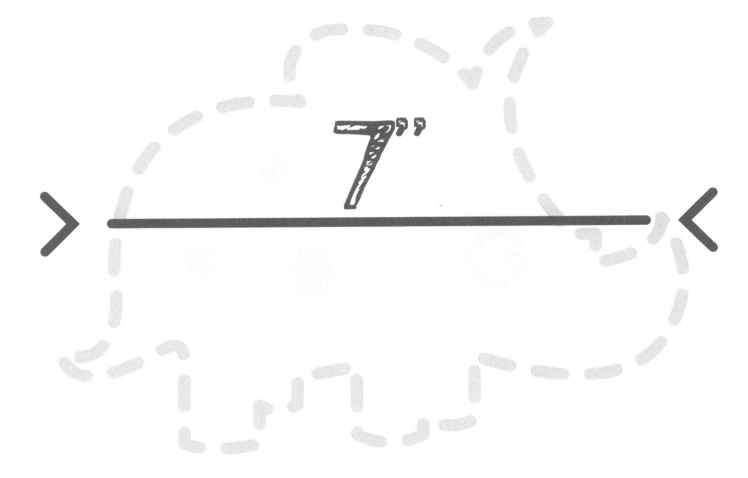

A World of
Dinos & Sports

Rex

Tri

Steggs

Bronto

Ptera

Bones

Cracked

Football

Hockey

Bowling

Basketball

Tennis

Trophy

Volleyball

Baseball

Pool

Soccer

Rexy

Big. Mighty. The King of Dinos is no small lizard.
With a loud ROAR, this guy gets everyone to
pay attention when he speaks.

Difficulty: Medium

Step
ONE

Create Basic Shape.

Step
TWO

Eyes & Spots.

WAIT

Step
THREE

Fill. You May Leave
the Eye Open.

Step
FOUR

Flip & Reveal.

Dino Foot

Rexy loves to Leave his mark everywhere
with these large footprints.

Outline Footprint.

Fill & Flip.

Tri

Horned nose. Big head.
This one is hard to miss
when he walks into any room.

Difficulty: Medium

Step
ONE

Create Basic Shape.

Step
TWO

Eyes & Spots.

WAIT

Step
THREE

Fill. You May Leave
the Eye Open.

Step
FOUR

Flip & Reveal.

Different Colored Eyes

Add some color to the eyes any of your Dinos.

Green Food Coloring

steggs

Spiky. Humped Backbone.
His armored plates keep him
safe during playful battles.

Difficulty: Medium

Step ONE

Create Basic Shape.

Step TWO

Eyes & Spots.

WAIT 30 SEC

Step THREE

Fill. You May Leave
the Eye Open.

Step FOUR

Flip & Reveal.

Volcano

Add some landscape to the plate
and watch the cheers explode.

Outline Volcano.

Fill & Flip.

Bronto

Long-Necked Leaf Lover.
This tall wonder is the cutest
of all the Dinos.

Difficulty: Medium

Step
ONE

Create Basic Shape.

WAIT

Step
TWO

Eyes & Spots.

Step
THREE

Fill. You May Leave
the Eye Open.

Step
FOUR

Flip & Reveal.

Give 'em Some Trees

Want to grow up big and strong?
Eat your greens like this Dino.

Outline Tree.

Fill & Flip.

Ptera

Flying high. Make sure you look above as this reptile takes flight with all his friends.

Difficulty: Medium

Step ONE

Create Basic Shape.

Step TWO

Eyes & Spots.

WAIT **30** SEC

Step THREE

Fill. You May Leave the Eye Open.

Step FOUR

Flip & Reveal.

Different Colored Spots

Add some color to the spots any of your Dinos.

Blue Food Coloring

Bones

Dig. Uncover a wonder.
Sadly, this one will be lost
again once he is in your belly.

Difficulty: Hard

Step ONE
Head & Eye.

Step TWO
Create skeleton body.

WAIT

30 SEC

Step THREE
Fill. You May Leave the Eye Open.

Step FOUR
Flip & Reveal.

Fossil Bone

Every Dino loves to play fetch.

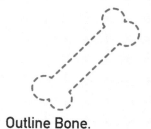

Outline Bone.

Fill & Flip.

Cracked

Big Spotted Egg. Each Dino cracked from a shell sure was cute from the start.

Difficulty: Medium

Step
ONE
Top & Bottom.

WAIT **30** SEC

Step
THREE
Fill.

Step
TWO
Create Spots.

Step
FOUR
Flip & Reveal.

Every Egg is Unique

Add some spots of color to your cracked Dino eggs.

Red Food Coloring

Football

30. 20. 10. 5. Touchdown!
Make a long run or catch a pass
for this game-winning treat.

Difficulty: Medium

Step
ONE

Basic Ball Shape.

Step
TWO

**Add Stripes
& Laces.**

WAIT

Step
THREE

Fill.

Step
FOUR

Flip & Reveal.

Kick a Field Goal!

This gridiron goal post is sometimes
the difference between a win or loss.

Outline Goal Post.

Fill & Flip.

Hockey

Stick. Puck. Net. Speed.
Put it all on ice and find out
the real challenge.

Difficulty: Easy

Step ONE

Create Oval.

Step TWO

Add Depth.

WAIT **30** SEC

Step THREE

Fill.

Step FOUR

Flip & Reveal.

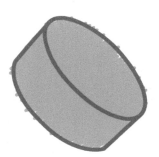

Score a Goal!

Take a shot and put the puck
in the back of the net.

Draw Net.

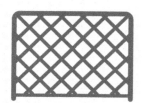

Flip.

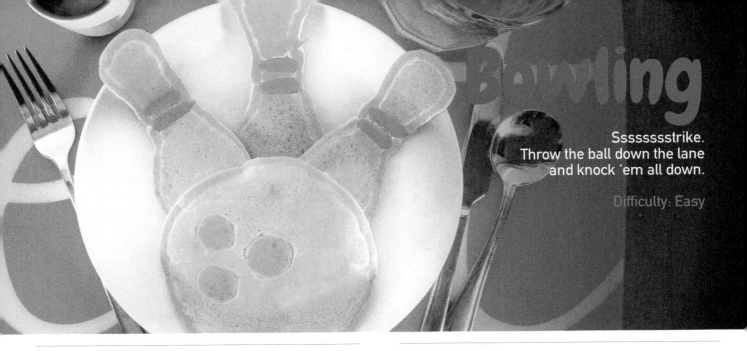

Bowling

Sssssssssstrike.
Throw the ball down the lane
and knock 'em all down.

Difficulty: Easy

Step ONE

Create Finger Holes.

Step TWO

Add the Circle.

WAIT 30 SEC

Step THREE

Fill. You May Leave
the Holes Open.

Step FOUR

Flip & Reveal.

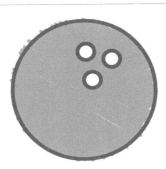

Get a Strike!

Set up these pins and knock down all 10.

Outline Pin.   Fill & Flip.

Basketball

Bounce or Pass this one on the hardcourt, but make sure to finish with a Slamdunk!

Difficulty: Easy

Step ONE

Create the Circle.

Step TWO

Add the Seams.

WAIT

Step THREE

Fill.

Step FOUR

Flip & Reveal.

Shoot it in the Hoop

Take a long 3-point shot. Swoosh!

Draw Net.

Flip.

Tennis

Forehand. Backhand.
Volley this tennis ball across the
net to challenge your opponent.

Difficulty: Easy

Step
ONE

Create the Circle.

Step
TWO

Add the Seam.

WAIT **30** SEC

Step
THREE

Fill.

Step
FOUR

Flip & Reveal.

A Grand Slam Racket

Give the ball a smash on the plate
with a simple racket.

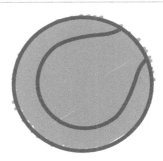

Draw Racket.

Fill & Flip.

Trophy

We are the Champions!
Savor a great season or
celebrate the winning goal.

Difficulty: Medium

Step
ONE

Create the Top Cup.

Step
TWO

Add Handles
& Base.

WAIT **30** SEC

Step
THREE

Fill Cup & Base.

Step
FOUR

Flip & Reveal.

Grand Podium

Take a stand as the grand ceremony begins.

Draw Podium.

Fill & Flip.

More Sports

  **Volleyball**

Bump.
Set.
Spike.

  **Baseball**

Watch it.
It's Loooooooong Gone!

  **Pool**

8 Ball Corner Pocket

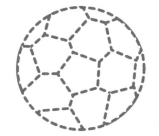  **Soccer**

Kick.
Goooooooooal.

LOL & OMG
Emojis

Kissy
Smiles
Silly
Tasty
Devilish
Cool
Love
Smirky
Shriek
Knockout
Grimace
Geek'd
LOL
Angel
Sad
Plain
Winky
Wowza
Alien

Kissy

A smooch on the cheek, or blowing
a kiss across the room to your loved one.
Start the day by giving that someone
special a big old kiss or two.

Difficulty: Medium

Step ONE

**Eyes, Brows
Lips & Heart.**

Step TWO

Create the Circle.

WAIT

Step THREE

**Fill. You May Leave
the Eye & Heart Open.**

Step FOUR

Flip & Reveal.

A Red Kiss

Give a lip-smacking kiss with some added color.

Red Food Coloring.

Smiles

Happy. How life should be every day.
Start someone's day off right
by just giving them a big smile.

Difficulty: Easy

Step
ONE

Eyes & Lips.

Step
TWO

Create the Circle.

WAIT

Step
THREE

Fill. You May Leave
the Eyes Open.

Step
FOUR

Flip & Reveal.

Say It with a Bubble

Make a few different emojis and
place them in a text bubble.

Rectangle Chat.

Oval Chat.

Silly

Laughs. Unexpected fun. Sometimes you have to let go and show your goofy side.

Difficulty: Medium

Step ONE

Eyes, Mouth & Tongue.

Step TWO

Create the Circle.

WAIT 30 SEC

Step THREE

Fill. You May Leave the Eye Open.

Step FOUR

Flip & Reveal.

The Eyes Tell It All

A wink or a crazy cross eyes. These will add some fun to your silly pancake.

Simple Silly.

Crazy Silly.

Tasty

Yumm. Hungry for more?
Give your crowd a lip-smacking treat.

Difficulty: Medium

Step ONE

Eyes, Mouth & Tongue.

Step TWO

Create the Circle.

WAIT

Step THREE

Fill. You May Leave the Eyes Open.

Step FOUR

Flip & Reveal.

Give a Thumbs Up

Show them how much fun you had last night.

Outline Hand.

Fill & Flip.

Devilish

Mischievous. Give a little grin.
Don't be cruel, but sometimes you
can have fun being a little devilish.

Difficulty: Medium

Step
ONE

**Eyes, Brows
& Mouth.**

Step
TWO

**Create the Circle
& Horns.**

WAIT

Step
THREE

**Fill. You May Leave
the Eyes Open.**

Step
FOUR

Flip & Reveal.

Pitch Fork

This guy needs his fork to poke
a little fun at those around him.

Outline.
(or just straight lines)

Fill & Flip.

37

Cool

Light & Bright. On a sunshiny day,
put on your sunglasses to look cool
- but always remember,
you're never too cool for school.

Difficulty: Easy

Step ONE

Eyes & Sunglasses.

Step TWO

Create the Circle

WAIT

Step THREE

Fill.

Step FOUR

Flip & Reveal.

Sunshine

Add a little sunshine to put
those stylin' sunglasses to use.

Outline Sun.

Fill & Flip.

Love

Ah, romance. Can't stop thinking about that special someone? Sometimes it really shows through in your eyes.

Difficulty: Medium

Step ONE

Heart Eyes & Mouth.

Step TWO

Create the Circle.

WAIT

Step THREE

Fill. You May Leave the Mouth Open.

Step FOUR

Flip & Reveal.

Add Some Hugs & Kisses

These letters always accompany a happy heart and love.

Draw a large 'X' and 'O' on the griddle. Flip.

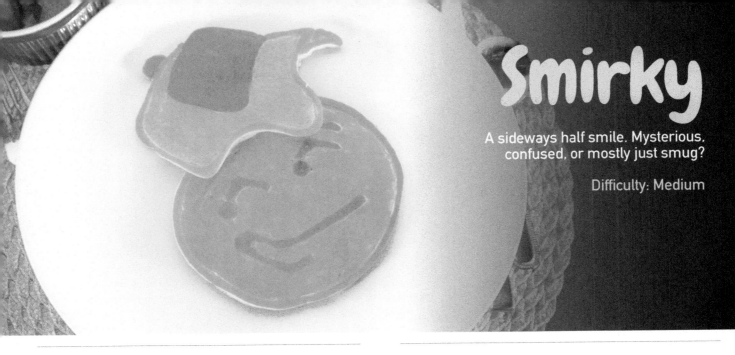

Smirky

A sideways half smile. Mysterious, confused, or mostly just smug?

Difficulty: Medium

Step ONE

Eyes, Brows & Mouth.

Step TWO

Create the Circle.

Step THREE

WAIT

Fill Completely.

Step FOUR

Flip & Reveal.

Add a Ball Cap

Make this hat to put on the top of this smug emoji look.

Outline Cap.

Fill & Flip.

Knockout

Sheer disbelief. This guy can hardly believe what just happened. Incapacitated from astonishment.

Difficulty: Easy

Step ONE

Eyes & Mouth.

Step TWO

Create the Circle.

WAIT

30 SEC

Step THREE

Fill. You May Leave the Mouth Open.

Step FOUR

Flip & Reveal.

Eyes of Expression

Change the comical knockout to tell a completely different story.

Sad Knockout.

Whoa Knockout.

Shriek

Shocked. Let out a loud shriek of surprise when something unexpected happens.

Difficulty: Medium

Step
ONE

Eyes, Mouth
& Hands.

Step
TWO

Create the Circle.

WAIT 30 SEC

Step
THREE

Fill. You May Leave
the Eyes Open.

Step
FOUR

Flip & Reveal.

Eeek... It's a Mouse!

Make a little mouse to shock
this shrieking emoji.

Outline Mouse.

Fill & Flip.

Grimace

Is it Freezing? Or maybe it's scared? Or is it just grinning
with a sense of the fun that's about to come?

Difficulty: Medium

Step ONE

Eyes & Mouth.

Step TWO

Create the Circle.

WAIT

Step THREE

Fill. You May Leave
the Eyes & Mouth Open.

Step FOUR

Flip & Reveal.

It's a Party. Surprise!

Make the celebration complete by
putting on this festive party hat.

Outline Hat.

Fill & Flip.

More Emojis

Geek'd

Cool Glasses.
Smart is Even Cooler.

LOL

Laughter.
Sheer Joy.

Angel

Sweet.
Always Perfect.

Sad

Bad Day.
Big Tear.

Plain

**You're Right.
I'm Wrong.**

Winky

**Nudge. Nudge.
Wink. Wink.**

Wowza

**Shocking.
Wow.**

Alien

**Distant Planet.
Bug Eyes.**

Tips & Tricks

Make Extras

Make an extra batch and store it in the freezer. This helps you prepare for last-minute breakfasts. Make-ahead meals are always a great option when you want to enjoy breakfast with your family or on the run.

Reheat in the toaster for the best results.

Warm Oven

At the lowest setting, place a cookie sheet in the oven. When a few pancakes are done, place them on the sheet to keep them warm while you keep making more pancakes.

Don't keep them in the oven too long as they will dry out. 15 minutes max.

Add Color

Use this tip when you want to get creative and really impress your crowd. Separate into different bowls. Add a few drops of food coloring, then bottle it up and use in your design. The results are amazing when you try more than one color. This is fun to do after you get your basic technique down. Imagine creating a colorful rainbow on a rainy day for your munchkin.

Make Ahead

If you think the next day will be hectic in the morning, your batter can be made the night before. Store it in the refrigerator, either in the squeeze bottles or in a bowl. You'll need to let the batter come to room temp (approx. 15-20 minutes) before getting to work. With any batter, the results are best right after mixing, as all the active ingredients react to the to griddle slightly better. Making your batter ahead doesn't affect the flavor at all, but it will save you time in the morning.

Add Flavor

If you want to switch up your syrup for another treat, try spreading a few other options instead. Jam. Jelly. Chocolate spread. Peanut butter. Marshmallow spread. Even cut fruit is enough to give your pancakes a twist of flavor.

Notes

How to Create Pancake Shapes: Dinos, Sports & Emojis Edition

Attending 'He & Me Bowling'
with one of my daughter's
Girl Scout events.

This book is dedicated to my daughters,
Isabella & Gabriella. I Love You!
Big Daddy

Look for more Big Daddy Pancakes cookbooks!
For more techniques & videos, check out:

www.bigdaddypancakes.com

CPSIA information can be obtained
at www.ICGtesting.com
Printed in the USA
BVOW05s1322081217
502326BV00010B/53/P

9 781364 244910